How Snakes Slither

BY EMMA HUDDLESTON

CONTENT CONSULTANT
DAVID HU, PHD
PROFESSOR
MECHANICAL ENGINEERING
GEORGIA TECH

Kids Core
An Imprint of Abdo Publishing
abdobooks.com

abdobooks.com

Published by Abdo Publishing, a division of ABDO, PO Box 398166, Minneapolis, Minnesota 55439. Copyright © 2021 by Abdo Consulting Group, Inc. International copyrights reserved in all countries. No part of this book may be reproduced in any form without written permission from the publisher. Kids Core™ is a trademark and logo of Abdo Publishing.

Printed in the United States of America, North Mankato, Minnesota
042020
092020

Cover Photo: Shutterstock Images
Interior Photos: Shutterstock Images, 4–5, 8, 12, 16, 21, 29 (middle); Marieke Funke/Shutterstock Images, 7; Kurit Afshen/Shutterstock Images, 10–11; Matt Jeppson/Shutterstock Images, 14, 15; iStockphoto, 18–19; Claus Lunau/Science Source, 23, 28, Ondrej Prosicky/Shutterstock Images, 24; Yuliya Yesina/Shutterstock Images, 25; Kristian Bell/Shutterstock Images, 26; Stephen Tattersall/Alamy, 28–29; P. Burghardt/Shutterstock Images, 29 (top)

Editor: Marie Pearson
Series Designer: Ryan Gale

Library of Congress Control Number: 2019954244

Publisher's Cataloging-in-Publication Data

Names: Huddleston, Emma, author.
Title: How snakes slither / by Emma Huddleston
Description: Minneapolis, Minnesota : Abdo Publishing, 2021 | Series: The science of animal movement | Includes online resources and index.
Identifiers: ISBN 9781532192975 (lib. bdg.) | ISBN 9781644944363 (pbk.) | ISBN 9781098210878 (ebook)
Subjects: LCSH: Children's questions and answers--Juvenile literature. | Snakes--Behavior--Juvenile literature. | Science--Examinations, questions, etc--Juvenile literature. | Habits and behavior--Juvenile literature.
Classification: DDC 500--dc23

CONTENTS

There are 35 species of garter snake.

CHAPTER 1

Unique Movement

A garter snake slithers along a grassy hill. Its body slides back and forth in an S shape. It moves quietly and smoothly over the ground. From above, only ripples in the grass give away its activity.

Moving without Limbs

Unlike many other animals, snakes don't have limbs. Snakes have to get around by moving only their bodies. Snakes can move their bodies in many ways.

A few snakes live in the water. These snakes are good swimmers. But most snakes live on land. Some can keep their bodies straight and scoot forward in a line. Others can move

Snakes Can Swim?

Most snakes live on land. But some live in water. They swim with a similar movement snakes use to slither on land. A water snake wiggles its body back and forth. Its tail pushes against the water to move it forward.

Sidewinder snakes throw themselves sideways to move.

forward by moving their bodies in an S shape. Some can even make the S shape to move sideways. When moving on land, a snake's scales play an important role in helping it slither along.

Some snakes are skilled climbers.

Snakes live in deserts, forests, oceans, and many other **habitats**. They climb up trees and slither over rocks and along the ocean floor. They can wriggle into tiny holes and cracks. More than 3,700 species of snakes exist around the world. Those that live on land push off the ground and use a winding movement to slither.

Explore Online

Visit the website below. Does it give any new information about how snakes move that wasn't in Chapter One?

How Snakes Move

abdocorelibrary.com/how-snakes -slither

Snakes use their belly scales to help them slither along many surfaces.

CHAPTER 2

Pushing off the Ground

Most land animals have limbs that push off the ground. This is how they move. But snakes are different. They do not have limbs. They have scales. Most snakes have scales covering their whole bodies. A few have scales only on their bellies.

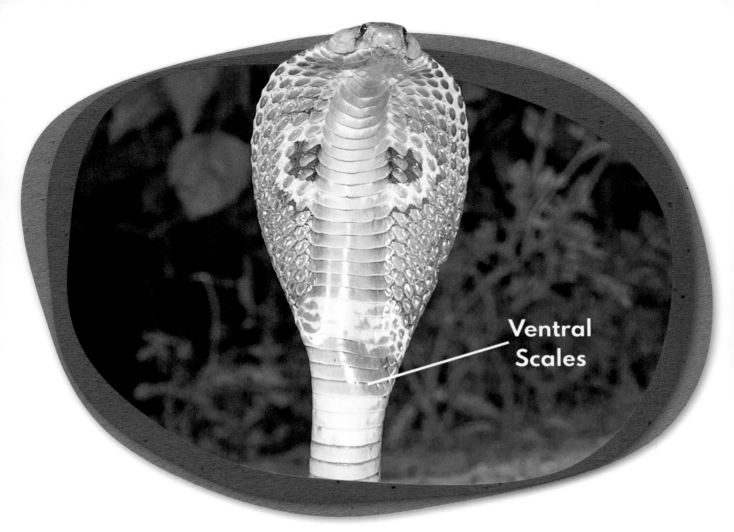

Ventral
Scales

Ventral scales stretch across a snake's belly.

Scales on the belly are called **ventral** scales. These scales are rectangular and wide. Their shape helps them grip the ground so the snake can push off and move forward. The number of ventral scales is the same as the number of ribs.

Ventral scales are angled back toward the snake's tail. This helps the snake's belly slide forward easily. The scales resist sideways or backward movement. This is because of friction. Friction causes the ends of the scales to catch against most surfaces.

Slick Scales

Snakes produce a thin, fatty coating that covers their belly scales. The coating makes the scales slippery. It protects them and helps them move smoothly while they slither over harsh surfaces such as rock, bark, and rough ground.

Snakes can use friction to move on many surfaces, including rock.

Friction

Snakes rely on friction to move. Friction happens when objects rub together. It causes surfaces to resist sliding across each other. It allows one object to push off the other in a certain direction.

Friction happens between a snake's body and the ground, a tree, or another surface. Scales help the snake grip and push off.

14

The sections of a snake's belly that touch the ground create friction.

Strong muscles help a snake climb trees or move on the ground.

Rough surfaces can be easier to move on. They have many bumps for scales to grip.

However, grip and friction are only part of the reason snakes can move. Slithering also requires snakes to use their muscles. Strong muscles let snakes move easily without limbs.

Further Evidence

Look at the website below. Does it give any new evidence to support Chapter Two?

What Is Friction?

abdocorelibrary.com/how-snakes-slither

A snake's skeleton is made of many small bones.

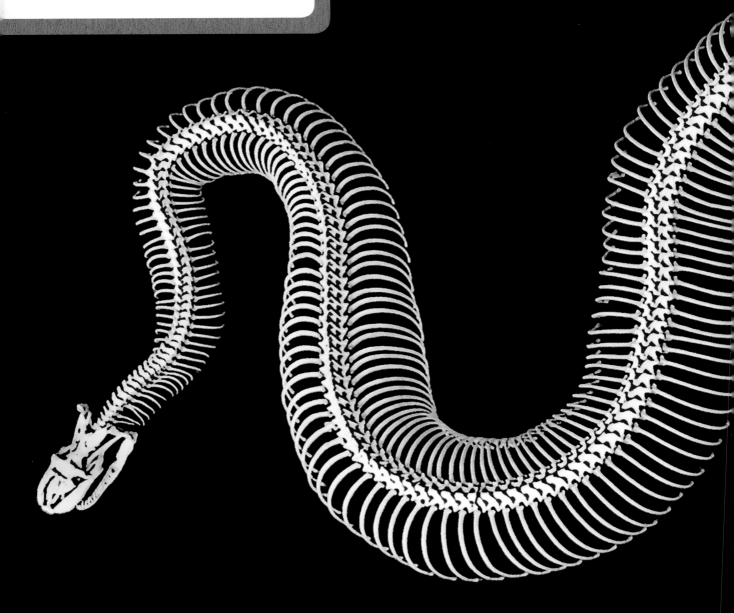

CHAPTER 3

The S Shape

Snakes can twist and coil their bodies. They are very flexible because they have many small bones and muscles. A large number of separate bones can bend more easily than fewer large bones. Being flexible helps snakes get around.

They can move in tight spaces, on thin branches, and more.

Slithering is a winding movement. A snake does it by **contracting**, or tightening, muscles. It tightens muscles on one side of the body. The contraction creates a **force** that pushes against the ground. The snake rapidly switches sides and repeats these movements. The forces from pushing off and tightening muscles cause the snake to move forward.

Ways to Slither

Snakes often slither in an S shape. They can slither in four different ways. The most common ways are serpentine and concertina. Serpentine movement starts at the neck. The snake's head

In serpentine movement, the body forms curves that look like the letter S.

swivels back and forth. Its body follows in that same winding path. The snake's ventral scales push off the ground. Serpentine motion is useful on land or in water. Most snakes use it.

Concertina movement is helpful for climbing. A snake reaches its head forward and sets it down as an anchor. The scales under its head grip the surface. Then it pulls the rest of the body up behind it, bunching it into an S shape behind the head. Once it sets its tail down, it can spring its head forward again to repeat the cycle.

A few snakes use sidewinding movement. Sidewinding is helpful on slippery surfaces such as sand. Snakes keep most of their bodies off the ground. They push off the ground at two points. They fling their bodies sideways.

Concertina Slithering

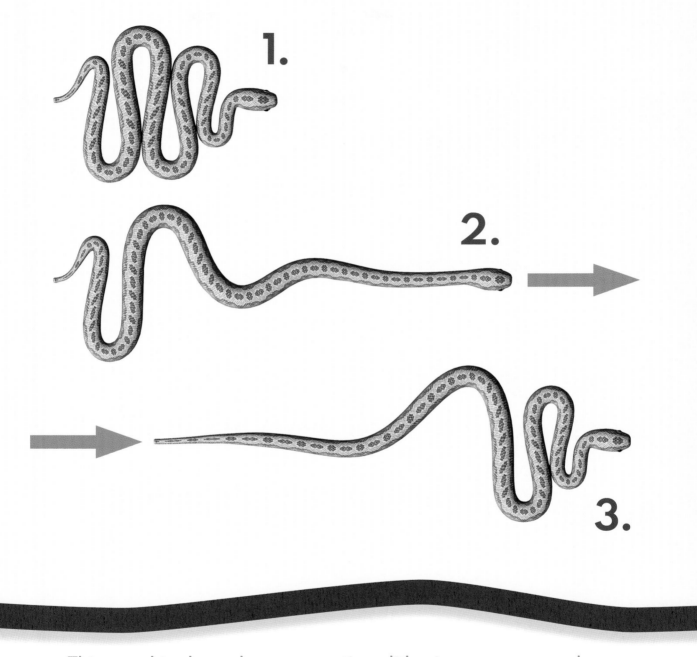

This graphic shows how concertina slithering moves a snake forward. The snake scoots its head forward. Then it bunches up its body toward its head.

Some sidewinder snakes live in the Namib Desert in southern Africa.

Another way snakes slither is through rectilinear movement. This is the slowest way a snake moves. The snake's body stays

Sidewinding Rattlesnakes

Some desert rattlesnakes slither sideways to get up hills. Sand is a difficult surface to move on because it shifts under weight. So the rattlesnakes sidewind to avoid sliding down a hill.

Large, heavy snakes most commonly use rectilinear movement.

fairly straight. Its belly curves up and down, not side to side. Parts of the body get lifted off the ground. The parts on the ground push forward.

Snakes can move easily on many types of surfaces.

Snakes are made to move, even if they don't have any limbs. Their scales, powerful muscles, and flexible skeletons let them slither along.

Primary Source

Gary Haith is a robotic engineer. He helped develop snakebots that would explore Mars. He said:

> A snakebot could navigate over rough, steep terrain where a wheeled robotic rover would likely get stuck or topple.

Source: Kevin Bonsor. "How Snakebots Will Work." *HowStuffWorks*, 19 Apr. 2001, electronics.howstuffworks.com. Accessed 28 Oct. 2019.

What's the Big Idea?

What is Haith's main point? Explain how the main idea is supported by details. Name a few of those supporting details.

Movement Diagram

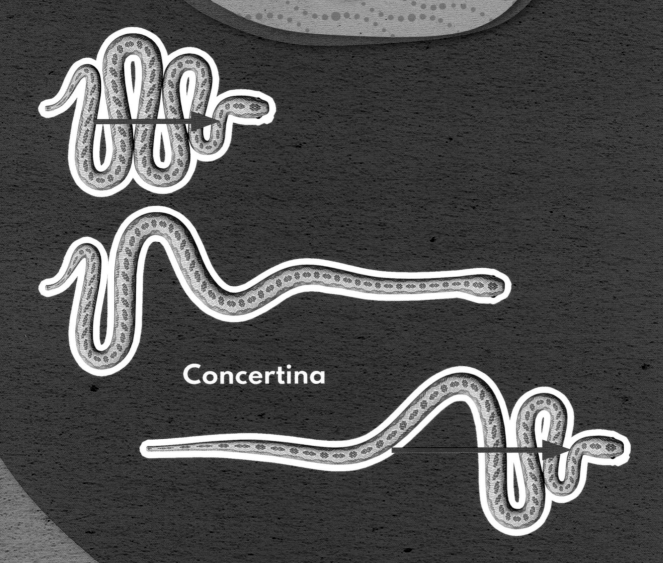

Concertina

Serpentine

Sidewinding

Rectilinear

Glossary

coil
to curl into a spiral shape

contracting
tightening

force
an action that can start, change, or stop an object's motion

friction
a force that resists movement when two surfaces come in contact

habitats
places where a species naturally lives

limbs
body parts such as arms and legs that branch out from the main body

resist
to work against movement in a certain direction

ventral
being on the underside or belly of an animal

Online Resources

To learn more about how snakes slither, visit our free resource websites below.

Visit **abdocorelibrary.com** or scan this QR code for free Common Core resources for teachers and students, including vetted activities, multimedia, and booklinks, for deeper subject comprehension.

Visit **abdobooklinks.com** or scan this QR code for free additional online weblinks for further learning. These links are routinely monitored and updated to provide the most current information available.

Learn More

Animal Planet Chapter Books: Snakes! Time, 2017.

Gish, Melissa. *Snakes*. Creative Education, 2018.

Hamilton, S. L. *Rattlesnakes*. Abdo Publishing, 2019.

Index

About the Author

Emma Huddleston lives in the Twin Cities with her husband. She enjoys reading, writing, and swing dancing. She thinks the science of animal movement is fascinating!